# _W_ild _&_ funny

## The most _amusing_ animal pictures ever

**Reading's Fun** LTD.

First distributed in 1995 in the
United States of America by
Reading's Fun Ltd
119 South Main Street
Fairfield, IA 52556

Produced by Weldon Russell Pty Ltd
107 Union Street
North Sydney
NSW 2060, Australia

A member of the Weldon International
Group of Companies

Chief Executive: Elaine Russell
Publisher: Karen Hammial
Managing Editor: Ariana Klepac
Editors: Megan Johnston, Kayte Nunn
Caption Writers: Susan Hurley, Jane Sheard
Designers: Silvia Martello, Catherine Martin
Picture Researcher: Anne Ferrier
Production: Dianne Leddy

© Weldon Russell Pty Ltd 1994

Printed by Tien Wah Press in Singapore

A KEVIN WELDON PRODUCTION

*endpapers:* macaroni penguins
*cover:* brown bear
*back cover:* snake-necked turtle
*page 1:* camel
*opposite title page:* flamingos
*opposite:* lioness and cubs

**Polar Bears:** Going flat out...
even watching exercise is exhausting.

**Emperor Penguin:** "Oh, what a feeling!"

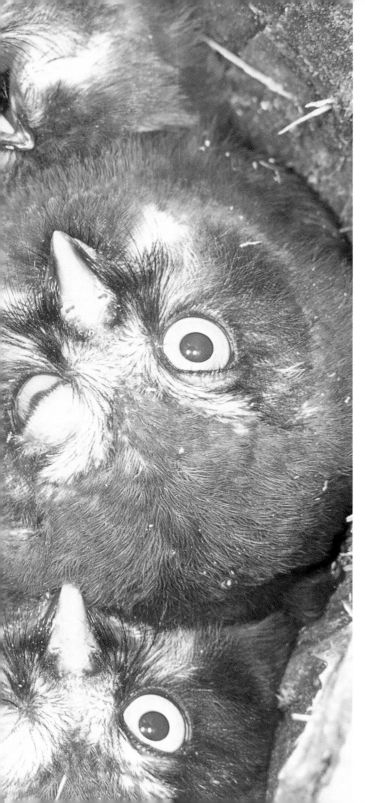

**Screech Owl Chicks:**
Don't trifle with this eyeful.

**Hippopotamus:** "Who are you calling weedy?"

**Snake-necked Turtle:** Feeling a little green around the gills.

**Pig**: All ears? Or hogging the conversation?

 **Bulldog:** Paws for effect when describing the family jowls.

**Penguins:** Following in father's footsteps.

**Hippopotamus:** Pink appearing when the big guy goes belly-up.

**Monkeys:**
Prima(te) ballerinas ...
entrechat ...

... jeté ...

... glissade.

**Baby Elephant:** Bath time – stretched out in de mud.

**Lion Cub:** Snooze time – stretched out on de mudder.

**Grizzly Bear Cub:** "What's bruin over there?"

"Bless my stars –
it's the Great Bear hug-in!"

"I wasn't invited. It's not fair ...
just 'cos I'm the Little Bear."
Grumble, grumble, grizzle, grizzle.

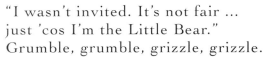

23

**Blacktail Prairie Dogs:** "Psst! Heard the latest gossip?"

**Sea Otter:** *"Don't otter another word! I don't want to listen ..."*

**Raccoon:** See no evil. "Can I look now?"

**Elephant Seal:** Speak no evil. "My lips are sealed."

**Australian Tree Frog:** "Aw, c'mon…I'm not as green as I look."

 **Giant Skink:** The final twist in the tail.

**Sharp-nosed Frog:** Diving force.

**Chimpanzees:** Facial workouts to preserve youthful ape-peal.

**Grizzly Bear Cubs:**
No-one will ever know –
did she fall or was she pushed?

**Salt-water Crocodile:** Salad dressing.

**Badger:** What on earth is she wearing?

**Grizzly Bear:** Letting it all hang out.

**Malayan Sun Bear:** Gaining a toehold.

**Chimpanzees:**
"Jump – I'll catch you."
"No, you come here – I'll pull you up."

**Australian Fur Seal:** Playing the flip side.

**Wild Turkeys:** Hen-pecked ... or talking turkey?

**Monkeys:** On your marks, get set...

**Lion Cub:** Not so steady, but ready to go.

**Adelie Penguins:** Measuring up.

**Ring-tailed Lemur:**
"My tail is *this* much longer than yours."

**Chimpanzee:**
"Get out of
town, redhead."

**Orang-utan:** "You haven't seen the last of me, chump."

**Wandering Albatross:**
Follow the leader – "One-and-two-and-three-and ..."

**Snowy Owl:** Not 'owling, singing.

**Mallard:** The snowbill effect – once one
flake sticks to the beak, the pile keeps growing.

**Emperor Penguin Chick:**
"I've been here so long I'm part of the scenery."

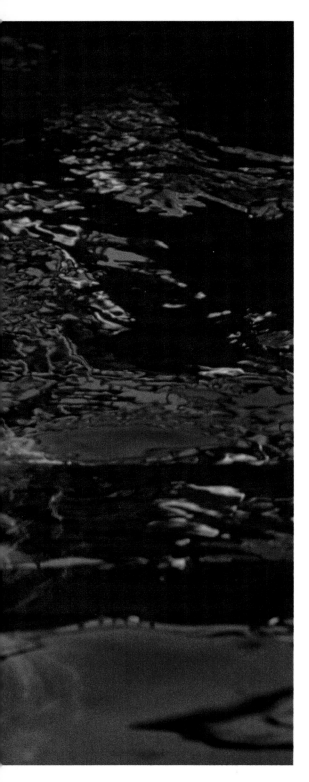

**Harbor Seal:** Wink or swim.

**Chinstrap Penguin:**
Smile and the whole world smiles with you.

**Elephant Seals:**
"My friend Flipper."

**Leaf Insect:**
"Leaf me alone or you'll make me cross!"

**Chameleon and Grasshopper:**
"Hang on – I'm about to change color."

**Grasshopper Mouse:** Serenading the stars.

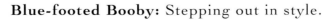

**Blue-footed Booby:** Stepping out in style.

**African Elephants:** Developing calf muscles.

**Polar Bears:** Roaring with laughter.

**Bornean Orang-utan:** Contemplating the hair and now.

**Saw-whet Owl:** "Eye's watching you."

**Crocodile and Butterfly:**
"Something's tickling my nose."

**Painted Turtle and Frog:**
"What's the trouble?
A frog in your throat?"

**Crocodile and Frog:** "Now, open wide."

**Terrapins:** Never let things get on top of you.

**Caiman Crocodile and Turtle:**
The balance of Nature –
as long as the croc
doesn't turn turtle.

**Baby Frigatebird:** The skinhead look – he'll grow out of it.

**Reddish Egret:**
"Je n'egret rien –
not even this haircut."

**Rockhopper Penguin:** Hopping mad.

**Burrowing Owl:** Best foot forward.

 **Afghan Hounds:** Pup-pet show is a howling success.

**White Cats:** Pail-faced but purr-pussful.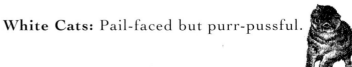

**Marine Iguanas:** Lounging lizards.

**Walruses:** Long in the tooth but not too old to fall in love.

**King Penguins:** Courtly love.

**Gray-headed Albatross
Chicks:** Bird-watchers
chick out the action.

**Caracal:** A good sense of hairing.

**Llama:** "Lend me an ear."

**Giraffe:**
"Necks one please!"

**Brown Bear:** Not hidden, but bear-ly visible.

**Mallards:** Telling tails –
they've ducked down
to the bottom.

**Giraffes:**
Stretching the point.

**Orang-utans:**
Stretching their legs.

**Young King Penguin:** A fine coating of fluff.

**Grizzly Bear:** Up to scratch.

**Hippopotamuses:** Grand passion.

**Lions:**
Taking love on the chin.

 **Geckoes:** Mouthing insults.

# Index

# Acknowledgments

Weldon Russell would like to thank the following photographic libraries for supplying pictures for reproduction:

Adventure Photo: p 91 (Kennan Ward).
Alaska Stock Images: p 34/35 (Johnny Johnson).
Animals, Animals: p 7 (right) (Gerald Kooyman); p 79 (Johnny Johnson).
Ardea: p 4/5 (Y. Arthus-Bertrand); p 39 (Kenneth Fink); p 55 (G. Robertson).
Auscape International: p 24 (Jeff Foott); p 25 (Jeff Foott).
Australian Picture Library: endpapers (Minden Pictures); p 6/7 (left) (Minden Pictures/Michio Hoshino); p 8/9 (ZEFA); p 14/15 (ZEFA); p 27 (ZEFA); p 51 (Evan Collis); p 60 (left) (Minden Pictures/Franz Lanting); p 67 (ZEFA); p 69 (Woodfin Camp); p 78 (bottom) (ZEFA/Charles Krebs).
Balthis, Frank S.: p 26; p 78 (top).
Barber, R. E.: p 53; p 72.
Bentsen, Steve: p 73; p 93 (Nolana McAllen).
Biofotos: p 71 (Brian Rogers).
Britstock-IFA: p 2, (Aberham); p 56 (Weststock).
Bruce Coleman: p 18/19 (middle) (Konrad Wothe); p 49 (O. Langrand); p 83 (Steve Kaufman); p 63 (M. Fogden).
Fogden, M. & P.: p 31.
Frank Lane Picture Agency: p 10 (Fritz Pölking); p 66 (R. Van Nostrand).
Greg Evans International Picture Library: p 82 (Chris Burrows).
International Photo Library: cover.
Kuhn, Dwight R.: p 68 (bottom); p 94/95.
McDonald, Joe: p 50; p 37 (J. Mustel); p 58/59.
McDonald, Mary Ann: p 88.

NHPA: p 21 (Nigel Dennis); p 42 (Anthony Bannister); p 61 (right) (Anthony Bannister); p 68 (top) (Martin Wendler); p 85 (Henry Ausloos).
Norbert Wu: p 36; p 46.
Oxford Scientific Films: p 12 (left) (Raymond Blythe); p 16 (Michele Hall); p 54 (Philipe Henry); p 64 (Martyn Colbeck); p 65 (Tom Ulrich); p 74 (Konrad Wothe); p 86/87 (Frank Schneidermeyer); p 89 (Konrad Wothe).
The Photo Library, Sydney: p 12/13 (right) (Robert Haddock); p 19 (right) (Cynthia Gaden); p 32 (R. Van Nostrand).
Photo Researchers Inc.: p 92 (Tom McHugh); p 90 (Robert Hernandez).
Planet Earth Pictures: p 11 (top) (David Maitland); p 18 (left) (Nigel Tucker); p 28/29 (left) (Mary Clay); p 47; p 48 (Norman Cobley); p 70 (Johnathon Scott).
Premaphotos Wildlife: p 43 (K. G. Preston-Mafham).
Prisma: p 2/3.
Stack, Tom & Associates: p 22 (left) (Thomas Kitchin); p 22/23 (Thomas Kitchin); p 23 (right) (Victoria Hurst).
Stock Photos: p 30 (Norbert Wu); p 33 (Dimaggio/Kalish); p 40/41 (Eddie Adams).
Stockshots: p 84 (Peter Robinson).
Survival Anglia: p 52 (Joel Bennett); p 62 (Dieter & Mary Plage); p 80/81 (Joel Bennett).
The Wildlife Collection: p 17 (Tim Laman).
Wildlight/Liaison: p 44/45 (Craig J. Brown); p 57 (Anne E. Zuckerman); p 75 (Dan Cox).
Wildlight Photo Agency: p 1 (Philip Quirk); p 29 (right) (David Moore); p 76 (Philip Quirk); p 77 (Philip Quirk).
Wildstock: p 38.